I walk in Faith that I am
a holy, chosen, redeemed,
dearly loved child of God
who is empowered by the
Holy Spirit, equipped by
God and enveloped by
Jesus.

A Heart
TO KNOW Him

When all you know to be true moves
from your head to your heart

Lynne Bauman

WestBow
PRESS
A DIVISION OF THOMAS NELSON

WestBow Press books may be ordered through booksellers or by contacting:

WestBow Press
A Division of Thomas Nelson
1663 Liberty Drive
Bloomington, IN 47403
www.westbowpress.com
1-(866) 928-1240

ISBN: 978-1-4497-6664-1 (sc)
ISBN: 978-1-4497-6663-4 (hc)
ISBN: 978-1-4497-6665-8 (e)

Library of Congress Control Number: 2012916430

Printed in the United States of America

WestBow Press rev. date: 09/27/2012

To my best friend, my husband.
You have been with me from the very beginning when God birthed this dream in my heart. You have loved and supported me through the entire journey. Your love for me and belief in me have carried me through.
Thank you for being there for me. Your support and guidance have given me the ability to see this God-sized dream to fulfillment.

My heart will be forever thankful.
All my love,
Lynne

Contents

Acknowledgments

- To my heavenly Father, who gave me a heart to know Him—Without Him, there would not be a book project. He alone birthed the dream, and He alone gave me the strength and the words to see it through. I cannot thank Him enough for the way He guided me through this process. Because of His great love for me, I want to live a life that is pleasing to Him.

- To my immediate family—my husband, Paul, and my children, David and Katie. I want you to know how very much I love you all. David and Katie, you are my pride and joy. I continue to believe in you both and trust God for the great plans He has for you.

- To my mom, dad, and brothers, Frank and Gerard— my life wouldn't be the same without you. Having all of you to share this dream with me makes it that much more meaningful and exciting. Mom, thank you for sharing in this journey with me. Your support and encouragement has been a precious gift.

- To my friend Lori—thank you for praying with me and leading me into a relationship with Jesus many years ago. Your efforts of discipleship were not wasted on me, as your labor of love continues to be one of the foundations of my walk with God.

- To my friend Brenda—how do I thank you for a lifetime of friendship? We are kindred spirits, and our friendship has deep roots that have withstood time and distance. Thank you for your belief in me and for your encouragement that gently but firmly guided me to put pen to paper. Your gift of friendship has been an invaluable treasure in my life.

- To all my family and friends who have traveled this journey with me—you have shared in my writings and encouraged me along the way. Each one of you is a precious gift to my life.

Introduction

*I*t was a moment I'll never forget. I remember where I was, where I was sitting, and the moment I knew I wanted what she had. I was sitting in a Bible study at my church; we were studying a series from Beth Moore titled *Believing God,*[1] and we were watching a video of her speaking on the segment "Knowing God." What caught my full attention and touched the deepest area of my heart was when she said, "I may not know a lot of things, but one thing I know for sure is who my God is." As I write this now, years later, I feel the same impact on my heart as I felt back then for the first time. It was at that moment I knew I wanted for my life what she had. I wanted that same confidence to be sure about who my God was, and I didn't have it. What that study showed me was I knew *about* God, but I didn't really *know* Him.

What you are about to read is my story, my journey, in developing a heart to know God as I know Him now. It shows how His plan and purpose for our lives will be revealed to us as we commit to know and seek Him. For me, I feel my journey is just beginning and that I am truly entering into all God has planned for me. From my current vantage point in life, I am able to see that all the detours, stumbling blocks, deserts, and mountaintops I have encountered along the way. They have made me who I am today and truly brought me full circle.

As a teenager in 1980, I wrote a poem that describes a heart that was searching. Searching for healing, hope, and inner peace.

If I could have one wish
To use anyway I'd like,
I'd wish for inner peace within.
To end all my pains,
To end all my struggles,
To untie all the knots which
Lie within me.

To reach that ultimate point
Where the problems all dissolve,
Where the pains all subside,
Where the struggles all let loose,

To find my inner self,
To find the real true person
I am …
Is what I hope to find.

Once I have found all this,
I would like to share it with others.

Thirty-two years later, I am ready to start sharing! Even then, I was seeking *A Heart to Know Him*; I just didn't know it yet!

Vulnerability has at times been difficult for me, but God has shown me that being real and sharing struggles and failures can help others to not feel alone. I felt alone in many of my struggles, and that is often the Enemy's number one strategy. The Enemy wants us to feel like we are all alone, that no one cares, that our struggles are specific to us, and that no one could possibly be going through similar circumstances. That couldn't be farther from the truth. You are not alone. God is *always* with you. God *cares* for you, and there are many who have gone through similar life experiences. If my story helps your heart move closer to this truth, then the journey has been worth it.

Woven throughout this book are devotionals that I have written, titled "Heart Reflections." They have been birthed through my own healing in developing a heart to know God. They are included for you to do just that—reflect. Reflect on God's truth, and at the end of each one is a "heart response." Once we have heard His truth, it requires some action on our part. Take your time with each response. Be honest before the Lord, and allow Him to work in your life.

My prayer for you, my fellow reader and friend, is that you would be encouraged in your own walk with God. Open up your heart, maybe even for the first time, to all He has for you, so that even now you would begin your own journey in developing *A Heart to Know Him.* Ultimately, I pray that you would begin to know Him like you never have before and seek Him with all that is within you. I promise that journey will be life changing for you!

Chapter 1

Heart Reflection: Healing of the Heart

"He heals the brokenhearted and binds up their wounds." Psalm 147:3

I feel it safe to say that everyone suffers from a broken heart at some point in life. None of us are spared from a journey of brokenness. We are all touched by it in some way.

Dictionary.com[2] defines *brokenhearted* as "burdened with great sorrow, grief, or disappointment; devastated, overwhelmed, destroyed, crushed, despairing or frustrated." Whatever our brokenness is, we must understand that it impacts our hearts and changes us. We often put up walls to protect ourselves from being hurt again. Sometimes, if you are like me, you may think your pain is healed, but your brokenness can leave scars and emotional baggage you may not know exists. But it can affect the way you are living or even *keep* you from living. The true culprit could be broken moments in your life that you never allowed God to heal fully. Circumstances and events can reopen wounds that reveal our brokenness. I want *all* of God's best for me and for you, and we shouldn't settle for anything less than that. God wants us healed and whole.

Much like the Israelites who wandered in the desert for forty years before reaching the Promised Land, we can do the same thing when we don't allow God's healing work to be fully completed in our lives. We get stuck in negative thought patterns and allow our emotions and circumstances to control us.

I have a junk drawer. I'm sure somewhere in everyone's home there is a junk drawer. In my junk drawer, I have a small container that holds a lot of odds and ends: paper clips, pins, miscellaneous screws and nails, leftover parts to a project, spare keys— you get the picture. Things I probably won't ever need, but I'm afraid to get rid of. In that same container is a magnet, and when I need to find something, I search for the magnet because usually what I'm looking for is attached to it. I see our hearts in much the same way as the magnet. Our hearts are the recipients of much love as well as heartache over our lifetime, not always in equal amounts. It's human nature for our hearts to hold onto the love and happy memories that come with it, but unfortunately, we hold onto the heartache and painful memories we've experienced as well. This combination shapes who we are. But we don't usually start to unpack or process any of the heartache or pain until we are well into adulthood. Whether we realize it or not, consciously or unconsciously, that heartache seeps into our everyday lives and relationships and affects our thought patterns and eventually our behavior. That is really the journey—to first recognize and then take active steps with God to heal our hearts.

Heart response: When we allow God into our hearts and lives to take up residence, "He will fulfill His purposes for us" (Psalm 138:8). Will you allow Him access to your brokenness?

My journey begins in my childhood home. Over my bed, I had a plaque that said, "What you are is God's gift to you. What you become is your gift to God." I am so thankful to my mom, who placed that plaque in my room and probably had no idea the impact it would make on my life. I must have read that plaque every day. I can still see it when I close my eyes; it was olive green with orange and yellow flowers, and the words were written in white. Those words were a seed God planted in my heart for His plan to unfold in my life.

I have always been a people pleaser. As far back as I can remember, my life has been marked by moments when doing the "right thing" was of utmost importance to me. So it stands to reason that as a teenager, when I surrendered my life to Christ, my life became about pleasing Him as well. Let me first explain what I mean by "surrendered my life" to Jesus. Another word for surrender is *relinquished*, which means to "give up" or "let go." I grew up going to church, but as I got older, I became more aware that God wanted to have a personal relationship with me. A relationship where I could share my cares and concerns with Him as well as allow Him to navigate the course of my life—just like Carrie Underwood's song, "Jesus, Take the Wheel," says. That's what I did. I came to a place of understanding that something bigger than I was missing from my life, and I was willing to give up my way of doing things. I let Jesus have control of my life, and He became the sole priority in and of my life. No longer did I want to make decisions without Him having a part in them, although I must admit there were still times when I would consult with God and went my own way anyway. The day I surrendered my life to Jesus, I came into a personal relationship with Him by acknowledging that God sacrificed His only Son to secure my salvation and that on my own I didn't have much to offer. But seen through Jesus' sacrifice, I became whole.

I was a freshman in high school and attending a Youth for Christ/Campus Life winter retreat when I made my decision to know Jesus personally. The decision was not made without some reservations. My biggest struggle was wondering what was going to happen to my high school friends and how my life would change. Typical for a teenager, my thoughts were all about me! There was a small part of me that just wasn't ready to give it all over. To some degree, I was happy with my life, but deep down, I knew there was something missing. My dear friend Lori, who was my next-door neighbor as well as a leader in the Youth for Christ group, sensed my struggle, and we spent some time talking. One of the things she said that stood out to me the most was quite simple: "God will take care of your friends, and don't worry about it." Simple words, but God brought tremendous peace to me through that statement. It was a turning point for me, and that truth enabled me to let go and trust God.

With that truth shared, we prayed together. I asked Jesus to "take the wheel." It was a huge leap of faith for me, but God proved to be faithful. Eventually, my focus shifted, and the concerns I had about my friends were no longer important as God brought new opportunities and new friends into my life. In one way, my journey was just beginning. But in another way, God was continuing to nurture the seed planted within me as a child—"What you are is God's gift to you." What I became—what I did with my life—was my gift to Him.

I'm reminded of taking piano lessons during my early teen years. My parents had bought a beautiful piano, and shortly afterward, I started taking weekly lessons. I must admit I was not disciplined enough to practice every day. Every week I would rush home from school to cram in a few minutes of practice before my lesson. My teacher could tell; I wasn't pulling the wool over her eyes. I didn't care for taking lessons very much, but there *were* times when I would play my songbooks on my piano and sing to my heart's content. I loved those times, and I'd like to believe they were a gift to my parents. There was no joy for them in having a piano that sat unused. The joy for them was me playing and using my lessons and talent. God has blessed each life with abilities, talents, and gifts. His joy is seeing them used for His glory to make something beautiful out of our lives.

So my decision to have a personal relationship with Jesus was made at that winter retreat.

The following morning, I can clearly recall the joy and lightness of heart I experienced—one of the best memories of my life! When we surrender our life over to Jesus, even with some fear and doubt, God is able to do so much more than we can think of or imagine. That morning, my journaling and love for writing began. I began to journal about how God met me in such a special way and gave me a missing piece to my heart. I was experiencing a love—His love—and a peace—His peace—like never before!

For as long as I can remember, I have enjoyed writing. At that time, I loved to write poems. My daily life as a teenager provided me with great experiences to write about. My writings mainly consisted of poems about relationships, boyfriends, love, and heartache. At the ripe age of thirteen, we think we know about everything, including love. Yet at the same time, we don't have enough life experience to deal with all the rejection and heartache! I seem to recall a lot of that—whether real or imagined.

Writing has always been cathartic for me. I enjoyed writing out my feelings and emotions. That is why journaling is so enjoyable to me—I am just able to write it all down. It's the one place where I can express just about anything. As my writing progressed from silly teen poems, I started to realize the power of my words, and God began to show me the gift of encouragement and blessing in the written word.

When I was sixteen, I wrote a Thanksgiving poem. My grandfather worked for a printing press company at the time. He had his own printing press in his basement, and he printed my poem for me to give to my family and friends. My mom still puts my poem out as a centerpiece for Thanksgiving every now and then. What a treasured keepsake my grandfather gave to me! Allow me to share it with you ...

A Thanksgiving Thought

Thanksgiving time is here again with all the fuss and bother,
And sometimes in the midst of this, we give little thought to
our Father.
Take the time to give thanks to His name,
And sorry for the times we used it in vain.
Give thanks for the earth, sun, and moon;
Give thanks for the days, which were made night and noon.
Give thanks to His Son, who showed us the way,
And taught us how to love each and every day.
Let us thank Him for each other,
For we are sisters and brothers.
Thank Him for our friends
And each memory that never ends.
Thank Him for the faith which makes it easy to believe,
For the gifts of love and joy we are open to receive.
Stop now and think what He has given to you,
And be happy and joyful you are among the chosen few.
So let it not be a bother for us to stop and pray,

To thank our heavenly Father on this Thanksgiving Day.

I also wrote "Christmas scrolls" to my family. They were heartfelt letters to share the real meaning of the season and to express the love I had for each of them. I saw firsthand how the words I had written breathed life into their own hearts and affirmed their sense of worth. We definitely shed some tears over them! What a blessing that was.

Another time I wrote a poem for my mom's sixtieth birthday. What a treasured keepsake for her. It has always brought me great joy when I knew I had touched someone's heart through my words. Words, whether spoken or written, can bring life to others. Words are very powerful, as we are reminded that the "tongue has the power of life and death" (Proverbs 18:21). The very words we speak can bring either life and healing or death and destruction. This is such an important truth to me because I have been the recipient of both types of words. And those experiences only fueled my passion to speak (and write) words—God's words—of encouragement, healing, and life to others. Let me pause here to say that whatever your God-given passion is, pursue it with all your heart, because God wants to use *it* and *you* for His glory!

Those were examples of blessing someone else with my words. I have a very vivid memory where words of encouragement were spoken to me. Those words played such an influential part in my heart and life. In my high school religious studies class, we were given an assignment to write about someone we admired from the Bible. I wrote my paper on the prophet Jeremiah. Initially, I really didn't know anything about him, but when doing the research on him, I realized we had more in common than I thought. And little did I know how the book of Jeremiah would play such a pivotal part in my journey with God years later!

We then had to give an oral presentation to the class. I can still see myself standing in the classroom and giving my presentation—the sun was streaming through the windows and my teacher, Sister Ellen, was leaning against the side of her desk while listening. But what stands out even more clearly is when Sister Ellen wanted to speak to me after class. She was not the warm and fuzzy type, so my heart definitely skipped a few beats when she wanted to keep me after class! To my surprise, she complimented me on a job well done, and on top of that, she gave me a gift! It was a glass paperweight, and etched in glass were the words, "Those who bring sunshine to the lives of others cannot keep it from themselves." I have kept that paperweight throughout the years, and it has always had a very prominent place in my home.

That moment stands out as a life-changing event where I experienced for the first time the feeling of approval, value, and worth for something I had done. That moment and "the words of life" spoken to me that day still remain with me, as it was the first time that I could recall someone believed in me and, dare I say, thought I had worth and purpose.

I'm not sure if my teacher ever knew what a gift she had given to me that day and the impact those words had on my life, but I have been forever grateful. The words we speak not only are powerful to bring life to others, but they also have the ability to give hope long after they have been spoken. The words Sister Ellen spoke to me that day have continued to breathe hope into my life long after they were spoken. That event is one of the many cornerstones that God has used in revealing Himself to me and healing my heart.

I've shared these memories for a few reasons. One is to help you to see how God has His hand on you before the very beginning of your life. Jeremiah 1:5 says, "Before you were born I *set you apart*." Isaiah 49:1 says, "Before I was born the Lord *called me*." You are no accident. Whether you were planned by loving parents or not, it is God that has formed you and called you in to His marvelous purpose. He has a story to tell through each of our lives.

Anything and everything we go through in life is never wasted. Romans 8:28 says, "And we know that in all things God works for the good of those who love him, who have been called according to his purpose." Ultimately, if we allow them, our circumstances can drain the life out of us or we can recognize that God wants them to shape us into the image of Jesus. Painful circumstances often serve as the catalysts to find our God-given purpose and passion.

Secondly, I want to encourage you in the gifts and talents God has entrusted to you. Romans 12:6 says, "We have different gifts according to the grace given us." 1 Peter 4:10 says, "Each one should use whatever gift he has received to serve others." What passion lies within you? What talent or ability has God given to you that really makes you feel alive and with purpose? In whatever your answers are lies the purpose God has for you. "So I ask you *to make full use* of the gift that God gave you" (2 Timothy 1:6 CEV). He wants you to *use* the gifts given to you to minister and encourage those He has placed in your life.

The gifts God has entrusted to you need to be developed and nurtured. We need them to be active in us. For example, when we don't exercise our bodies, our muscles get weak and lose muscle mass. Once we begin to exercise, our muscles become stronger and bigger. Step out and begin to use the gifts and talents He has placed within you. Even if it's just a small step, it's a beginning. And when you do, God will be glorified through you!

Jer. 24:7

Prov. 4:23 — NIV

Living Prov. 4:23 —

NLT Prov. 4:23

Chapter 2

Heart Reflection: What Do You Believe? (Part 1)

"And how much more valuable are you than birds." Luke 12:24

*E*leanor Roosevelt said, "No one can make you feel inferior without your consent."[3] I've read the quote before, and to be quite honest, I have struggled with its meaning. After pondering it for some time, I found myself asking, "Why would you give someone consent to make you feel a certain way?" How foolish! And yet I faced the harsh reality that I have done that exact thing more times than I'd like to admit. As I continued meditating on this thought, I felt God give me this revelation: "You must believe, to some degree, that it's true." This was difficult to take in. I was completely blown away by the truth that was revealed. The negative thoughts I allow to bombard my heart are because, somewhere deep down, I believe them to be true.

For some strange reason, it is easier to believe something negative about ourselves or what others think of us. It's like the old pair of sweatpants, sweatshirt, or whatever your comfort clothes are. They may not be very flattering or even look that nice, much less give an accurate picture of what you look like, but they feel so good. They're comfortable clothes. In the same way, we have allowed ourselves to wear the negative perceptions of ourselves that others placed upon us, and that we have heard all along.

> "Why can't you do anything right?"
> "You could have done better."
> "You probably won't amount to much."
> "Why can't you be like your brother (or sister)?"

Instead of rejecting these negative images that have been put on us, we wear them like those comfortable old clothes. It becomes who we are. Possibly the deception comes in the things you may have *never* heard:

> "I love you."
> "I believe in you."
> "I'm so proud of you."
> "You have so much to offer."

Even silence can deceive us and strip us of our value, or maybe you have heard these words but don't believe them, and you revert back to the old, comfortable clothes.

How much harder is it to believe the truth from the God who created us? We are of *great* value to Him! This quote by William Gurnall, an English author and clergyman from the 1600's, can shed some light as to why we struggle with this issue: "We fear man so much, because we fear God so little."[4] We place more value in the words of others about ourselves than in the truth of God's Word. When we entertain negative thoughts of ourselves, whether from others or self-inflicted, I know this saddens the Father's heart. He created us, and His Word says that "everything He made was very good" (Genesis 1:31).

It all comes down to what you believe. You were created in the image of God! Don't believe or entertain the lies anymore. Your feelings, failures, and mistakes will never change God's view of you! Allow your heart to dwell on the one who created you and has bestowed great worth on you.

Heart response: Don't be so quick to give your consent away! "You are worth more than many sparrows" (Matthew 10:31).

I grew up in a family of five that included my mom, dad, and two brothers—one older and one younger. If you've ever read anything on birth order, I seem to have most of the typical traits of a middle child. Peacemaker, feeling life wasn't fair, feeling unloved and being adaptable. I've come to realize that a lot of the baggage we bring with us from childhood into adulthood can be both real and imagined. By *imagined,* I mean how we perceive things. That statement alone has helped me to see things through a different lens. For whatever reason, we sometimes perceive things much differently than how they actually happened, and we can contrive motivations from a skewed perspective that can often be unfair. Nonetheless, this is an important point to ponder when reliving childhood issues.

Being the middle child and only girl certainly had its pluses. I often got special attention, and being the only granddaughter on my father's side of the family brought its benefits as well. I know I was treated differently just by being the "only girl." There was specialness to it. And even in spite of the love and care I received, I still grew up struggling with low self-esteem, self-worth, insecurities, fear of rejection, and an insatiable need to be accepted and loved.

My brothers and I have many similarities, but we also couldn't be more different in some ways. My older brother, Frank, is a free spirit—he always did what he wanted, when he wanted, and if he was told something, he did just the opposite. This is no hidden fact. He will admit that to this day. Being a free spirit (code for rebellious!) certainly brought its share of problems for him and my parents. I saw what my parents were going through, and I didn't want to cause them any further upset. I became a caretaker of my younger brother, Gerard, in the sense that whenever there was any conflict going on in the home, I took him away from it. I would distract him, played games with him, etc. I felt like I was always trying to make peace and make everyone happy. I was the people pleaser, and this is something that has followed me throughout my life, often to my own detriment.

Gerard, I feel, marches to the beat of his own drum. Like me, he's not much for confrontation, but I think he has managed to avoid the overwhelming need to please others that I have struggled with. At home, my need to please others became a simple equation: if I pleased my parents, they would love me. My home had a lot of rules, and I was often plagued with fear and guilt if I broke those rules. When we got into trouble and were reprimanded by my parents, it not only came with consequences but silence. At least that was my perception. I perceived that silence as a temporary withdrawal of their love. I craved my parents' love and approval and lived most of my childhood and early adult life trying to gain it. As in any family, there are many highs and lows throughout a lifetime, but through them all and in spite of them, my family means the world to me. Family has always been a priority for me. And in spite of the many different roads we have traveled down, it will continue to be a priority to me.

I share some of my family dynamic to highlight how it all plays a part in our view of God, our concept of Him, and to see how it relates to what we believe. Our family interaction often models how we interact with God and view Him. This was never clearer to me then when I became a parent myself. I recall putting my children to bed and, as was our routine, they would say their prayers while I would finish. I don't remember my son's exact words, but one time he began his prayers as "Dear Mommy." At that moment, it clicked for me that at that young age, their concept of God was their parents! Doesn't this put parenting in a whole new light? To realize that your children view you as God and their future view of God will be shaped by this view—it's overwhelming! They can't help but to do that. The ways in which we were raised and the view we had of our parents is definitely connected to the kind of relationship we have with God and how we view Him.

Regardless of the baggage you come with into your relationship with God, you must see and believe Him for who He is. In knowing who He is, you will come to know how invaluable you are to Him. I can honestly say that the woman behind these words is not the same girl I was in high school. I could not be more different, and it is only because of God's generous grace and His redeeming transforming power in and upon my life. I could not be surer of the reason for this change. I became intentional in seeking after God with an earnest desire. Only in doing so did I begin to see the worth and value God had bestowed upon me and my life. He feels the same about you.

When my son was in high school, he played on the lacrosse team. Right before the start of every game, the team would huddle up for some last-minute encouragement from their coach. The team then shouted in unison, "Do work!" I believe this phrase meant they weren't going to play well or win without applying the efforts they had been trained in. They practiced hard and they played hard. In my son's senior year, their hard work had paid off as they secured the championship for their division!

The same thought applies to our relationship with God. We just don't come into a relationship with Him and then sit and do nothing. We don't fold our arms across our chest and blink our eyes in order for Him to answer our prayers. We have to seek God out and *grow* in our relationship with Him. It does take effort and discipline. I read a lot of inspirational books and studied on the areas of my weaknesses: forgiveness, healing, and significance, just to name a few. I spent time in prayer and reading God's Word to find the answers for my healing. Over time, I learned to *let go* of a lot of issues. But more importantly, I began to learn more about who God was and who I was as His child.

Even though I am far from the person I once was, I know that I'm still on the journey. The pain of someone's thoughtless words still sting, the lack of someone's care and concern still disappoints, and the truth that your expectations may not be someone else's still discourages. Most times, I am able to look through a healthy lens and not take on the hurt and disappointment. The reason for that is simply because I know that my heavenly Father loves me beyond measure and He's always on my side. That is the anchor we must hold onto when we are threatened to give our consent away, when we are tempted to give in to the lies that threaten to bring us under.

Early on in my relationship with the Lord, my perception of God was all about rules, right and wrong, and that if I did the right things I could earn His love. Much of my adult life was striving to earn God's love. I have always known that His love is unconditional, but this was only head knowledge. It took many years to fully accept that there is nothing I can do to earn it or make Him love me more. His love for me has always been and always will be. I just never believed it was for me and couldn't receive it for myself.

I spent a lifetime feeling like a failure, like I never quite measured up to *what I should be* and feeling like I always had to be better. Whew! What a way to live. And what consent I gave away to allow myself to believe this lie for all those years.

Chapter 3

HEART REFLECTION: WHAT DO YOU BELIEVE? (PART 2)

"Then you will know the truth, and the truth will set you free." John 8:32

This verse is the antidote when we are struggling with brokenness and the circumstances that cause painful experiences in our lives. We need to keep reminding ourselves that the truth *will always* set us free. God's truth sets us free. God's truth brings revelation, and although at times it may be difficult to accept, it is only for our betterment. After all, there may be some truth behind the negative thoughts you struggle with. But the negative thoughts, emotions, and hurtful words only bring condemnation—a sense of disapproval and blame—and only serve to make us feel worse about ourselves than we already do. The Holy Spirit's guidance and teaching can gently bring it into the light, help us process it, and allow His revelation to set us free. This is conviction, not condemnation. Ask yourself what painful mistruths you have been holding on to. What shame or hurtful experience has skewed your perception of life and allows you to only look through a lens of negativity? What words spoken to you have you kept anchored to your heart?

I once heard someone say, "If you walk through life with your psychological skin really burned and never heal it up, it doesn't take much to get to you. You are very pain sensitive. You need to figure out a way to heal your psychological skin." Hurtful words can be damaging. They leave scars that can take a lifetime to heal, scars that we are carrying around. Is your "psychological skin" wounded and in need of healing? There is hope; there is good news! God wants to pour His healing balm over these hurts, but that requires us to deal with the truth at hand and not run from it. And in order to deal with it, you need to know what you believe … you need to believe truth. Only by knowing who you are in Christ are you able to say, "I'm not going to receive that painful word or entertain that negative thought." Our brokenness needs to be viewed in light of who we are in Christ. Handling our hurts in this manner, God's way, brings revelation and freedom, not condemnation.

Heart response: May you truly *know and believe* the truth—God's truth—and allow it to set you free! His revelations are life changing!

There was a point in time when I was very afraid that I had lost my gift to write, because for a time I just stopped writing. I don't think it was for any reason other than the changes in my life. After graduating high school, I went away to college, and shortly after that, I got married. A few years after that, I started a family. Although journaling during my personal quiet times with the Lord continued, creatively I didn't do much, and I recall how that always nagged at me.

But words have always come easily for me whether verbally (as my husband will attest by letting me know I've used up all my words for the day!) or written. I have always had a freedom in expressing my heart and feelings on paper. As I've said, I've always enjoyed writing letters and cards of encouragement to family and friends. I have seen for myself both the liberating and detrimental affect the power of words can have on our lives and affect our hearts. We should be very mindful of the words we use, whether written or spoken, because they can either speak life to someone or speak destruction, which can leave one's heart broken and bruised. Proverbs 16:24 says, "Pleasant words are a honeycomb, sweet to the soul and healing to the bones." Proverbs 25:11 says, "A word aptly spoken is like apples of gold in settings of silver." And lastly, Ephesians 4:29 says, "Do not let any unwholesome talk come out of your mouths, but only what is helpful for building others up according to their needs, that it may benefit those who listen."

Scripture is full of admonitions to watch our speech and our tongue, and we would be wise to obey them. When you have experienced someone speaking life to you (like Sister Ellen, my religion teacher), first, you'll never be the same, and second, you'll realize the blessing in sharing words of life with others. Words hold the power of love, healing, and forgiveness as well as pain, sadness, and discouragement.

It just so happens I had such an experience while writing this book, and it threw me because my actions seemed so hypocritical. But God, through His precious grace, showed me how it all fits and is all part of my journey. But more importantly, He showed me that He doesn't wait for us to have it all together to use us.

The situation was with my then eighteen-year-old son who, as is typical with most teenagers, wanted more independence. I was struggling to hold on. Some events happened that caused me to harbor some hurt toward my son, and it was only a matter of time until I exploded and said some hurtful things to him in the process. Honestly, I was unsympathetic to what he was dealing with in his own life and I was just set on getting my point across. Well, I can proudly say I got it across, but at what a price!

After the damage was done, I was left to grapple with how to resolve it. Being wrong is not something that comes easily to me—admitting I'm wrong is even harder. Dr. Phil penned the phrase, "Do you want to be right, or do you want to be happy?"[5] Unfortunately, for most of my life it has been all about being right. There have been many wasted years of struggling to be right at the expense of my own happiness, but not this time. I cried out to God for strength to make the situation right. It was one of the most difficult struggles I ever had, mostly because I fully understood the consequences of my actions—I had hurt my son. God in His infinite mercy and grace gave me the strength to call my son. Through my many tears, I said I was so sorry for the things I had said and asked for his forgiveness. He replied, "Mom, chill. It's okay. Yes, I forgive you." And at that moment, the chains that had me bound were set free.

I encourage you to choose your words carefully and choose to speak life to those around you. You'll be so glad you did! It bears reminding that this is not something we can do on our own strength. We are human, and in the midst of trying situations and frustrating circumstances, we usually come up short on our own. But when we surrender and acknowledge to God that we can't do it on our own, His Holy Spirit comes in and gives us what we need: "His grace is *more than* sufficient for you" (2 Corinthians 12:9) Shortly after the phone call with my son, he sent me a text message that I will forever save. It read, "Mom, it's ok … we all get a little heated sometimes, but through it all I'll always love you and you can always be forgiven!" From a son who doesn't like to express himself emotionally too often, he spoke words of life, love, and forgiveness to me. Those are the same gifts that our heavenly Father gives so freely to us. How can we help but to give those same gifts freely to those in our life? "Freely you have received, freely give" (Matthew 10:8).

Words of love—like my son's text message and, even more importantly, God's Word—create truth to our hearts in difficult moments of life. His truth reminds us of who He is.

- He is the God of the impossible—nothing is too hard for Him.
- He is the God who never leaves you.
- He is the God who loves you unconditionally.
- He is the God whose peace passes all understanding.
- He is the God who works all things for your good.
- He is the God who heals and restores.
- He is the God who forgives and remembers your transgressions no more.
- He is the God who is the strength of your life.

These truths are promises from God's Word. His Word is his love letter to us, His children, and it is rich with the words of life, love, mercy, grace, forgiveness, freedom, redemption, restoration, peace, truth, strength, and hope. Reading it, praying it, and *believing* it to be alive and at work in our lives are the best ways to develop a heart that knows God. I have been reading the Bible since I was in high school, but only in the last several years have I been reading it with a new clarity, understanding, and belief. It has been life changing and has set me free from years of bondage!

Spend time getting into God's Word—start today! Ask the Holy Spirit to breathe a new clarity, understanding, and belief into you as you read it. For there your journey to developing a heart to know God will take root! His *truth* will set you free!

All the facts we
believe transfers to
our heart

Sets us free to transforms us,

God is the power outlet
we are the lights

Chapter 4

HEART REFLECTION: HE KNEW ME

"How great is the love the Father has lavished on us, that we should be called children of God! And that is what we are!" 1 John 3:1

There are times in our walk with God when we are seeking a breakthrough and we have to ask ourselves some questions. As I continue to yield areas of my heart over to God, He has been faithful to provide His healing touch. I had to ask myself some difficult questions to really get to the heart of the matter.

- Why do I continue to strive to get it all right?
- What motivates me to do what I do: fear or love?
- What defines my worth?

Have you ever experienced reading God's Word many times over or even heard it spoken in church and it doesn't make an impact? Then one day the Holy Spirit brings revelation? That happened to me while I was reading Galatians 1:15: "But when God, who set me apart from birth and called me by His grace." I stopped dead in my tracks and thought, *What did I just read?* It was as if the words had literally jumped off the page: "But when God, who *set me apart from birth.*" There is something about those words that just grabs at my heart! The Amplified Bible translation says, "But when He, who had chosen and set me apart *(even) before I was born* and had called me by His grace." Jeremiah 1:5 says, "Before I formed you in the womb I *knew* you; *before* you were born *I set you apart.*" And lastly, Isaiah 49:1 says, "*Before* I was born the Lord called me; from my birth He has made mention of my name." I was reading these Scriptures as if I were reading them for the first time, and the impact they made upon my heart was huge!

I continued to meditate over these verses, and I don't think I can adequately describe to you what took place in my heart. God brought such revelation, peace, and freedom to me. The revelation: He knew me—God set me apart from birth—before He formed me in the womb. He *knew* me! This means I was of great worth in His eyes, even before I had life! This same powerful truth applies to you as well!

What this truth allows us to see is that God knows you, chooses you, and sets you apart before you were *even* born. This reveals the great and immeasurable worth and value He has placed upon you even before you were a twinkling in your parents' eyes. Anything you are carrying from your past or experiencing in the present that is contrary to this truth has no hold over you. *He knew you! He knew me!* You are of great worth. Allowing this truth to permeate any broken place in your heart or any broken moments in your life will bring healing to your heart. This truth will restore your value and your worth, and it will make the days you are living more purposeful.

What this truth also reveals is that someone else's expectation of you does not define who you are, nor do our own perceptions of ourselves. Other people's view of you and your own view of yourself are distorted. Regardless of our failures and circumstances, we need to see ourselves through God's lens. He doesn't see you as you are today—He sees us whole, restored, and perfect in His eyes. The truth is that God *knew me* and He *knew* you, and that, my friend, changes everything! "You are of greater worth than many sparrows" (Luke 12:7 AMP).

Heart response: "He knew me" Write that upon the slate of your heart and allow that truth to change the perception of who you *think* you are.

I am no surprise to God.

My husband, Paul, and I got married when I was twenty-one. We met through the Youth for Christ ministry. I was so happy to have met someone who shared the same beliefs I had. Early in our relationship, we went to my senior prom together, and a few days after that, a classmate asked me if I was going to marry him. I said yes! It was just something I knew. One thing that always had attracted me to him, other than the fact that I loved him and wanted to spend a lifetime with him, was that he had a wonderful sense of humor and could always make me laugh. That ability to laugh and make each other laugh has gotten us through twenty-eight years together! After sharing all those years together, he truly has become my best friend.

But even our dating and engagement were not without some bumps in the road. As every parent has some reservations about the ones their children date, my folks were no exception. As you know, pleasing my parents and making them happy with me was always of top concern, until my decision to get married. It was the only time in my life, up to that point, that I made a decision based on what I wanted and what would make me happy and not anyone else. That was a pivotal moment in my life. But it wasn't easy. God's Word says to "honor your parents—which is the first commandment with a promise—that it might be well with thee" (Ephesians 6:2–3). I will be forever thankful to one of my bridesmaids, Gigi, who pointed that out to me. In the difficult times I was having, I needed to honor my parents. I worked this through with them, and in doing so, I obeyed God. It was not at all easy, but I believe there has been definite fruit in my life because of that decision.

Five years after we were married, we decided to start our family. Soon after, we welcomed our son, David, who entered the world at a whopping eleven pounds and twenty-two inches! (My body has never been the same!) My heart began to love in ways it never had before. He had captured it. Three years later, we welcomed our daughter, Katie, who entered the world at a dainty nine and a half pounds and twenty-one inches! My heart was now complete. They are both the joys of my life, and the memories of their childhood are very treasured ones. They made being a mom a great joy and it was something I felt came easy to me.

During those years of raising our children, I poured my life into them and feel that I gave them the love and attention I was seeking myself from God. Although my love for them was real, the expectations in raising them were all based around perfection. Looking back, I can see the expectations of perfection that I placed upon them. I had promised myself I wouldn't do that to my own children. Unfortunately, we often fall back on what we know. But even when we are aware, it is difficult to break the cycle. I think I did that in some ways, only by God's strength. Only by much prayer and by His strength was I able to make some progress, but it continued to be an ongoing struggle.

At this time, I hadn't really discovered who I was in God. My lens was distorted in thinking that I could only raise my children the right way by being perfect and that in doing so I would please God. Unfortunately, I spent many years of striving to please God through performance. I hadn't yet come to the realization that His view of me was not based on my performance but on my worth in Him. I came to understand that the Bible is filled with a cast of characters who were constant failures, and yet God's love for them was unchanging; He used them mightily to move His kingdom forward. Thankfully, God doesn't wait for us to have it all together, because we never will this side of heaven. He uses us in spite of ourselves to be a reflection of Him. Only by

His grace does He equip us with what we need when we turn to Him. When I began to discover and accept who I was in God, my relationship with God began to grow the most.

Let me explain what I mean when I talk about *knowing who you are in Christ*. Back when my children were in their teen years, we had a favorite saying we shared with them every time they left to go somewhere. As they headed out for their night's plans, my husband and I would say to them, "Remember who you are." I'm not quite sure where it came from—I think it was something we came up with to remind them not to make any foolish decisions.

I remember one time my husband explaining the saying to our daughter. "What we mean is to remember the family name. Remember that your decisions will affect your family." It also said to them that we were there for them. I know there were things that they kept from us, but still they knew they could come to us for help.

As they got a little older, I remember tweaking the saying a bit. Along with "Remember *who* you are," I added, "And remember *whose* you are." They were God's children, and I wanted to remind them that their behavior should reflect who they belong to. When my husband was particularly concerned about what they may be doing, he would remind them, "Remember who *I* am!"

Years ago, one of our pastors gave a sermon titled "You Bear the Name." It was such a great reminder that, as God's children, we bear His name wherever we go. We take Him with us, and in doing so we can call on Him whenever we need Him. It is that same reminder I gave my own children: Remember whose you are. We belong to Jesus. May our lives reflect that.

This is what we can be confident of as God's children:

- As His children, we find forgiveness.
- As His children, we find a love everlasting and unconditional.

- As His children, we find our future is secure.
- As His children, we find a peace that passes all understanding.
- As His children, we find the power of the Holy Spirit alive in us.
- As His children, we find redemption and restoration.
- As His children, we find all our needs supplied.
- As His children, we find we have the mind of Christ.

Knowing to whom we belong gives us the freedom to walk in these truths when we find ourselves in difficult situations, painful times of life, brokenness, and disappointments, as well as when life doesn't seem to be matching our own expectations.

This is why it is so important to have the Word of God hidden in our hearts—so we can stand upon it in our time of need. I have Scripture verses written everywhere. I write them down on random scraps of paper, in my journal, on my iPad—they are everywhere! And when I read them, not only do they often apply to the situation at hand, but they go down deep into my very soul and minster to my heart at my point of need.

The more we know who we are in Christ and accept that truth as our very own, the more our behavior will reflect what we believe. What healing that brings to one's heart!

Chapter 5

HEART REFLECTION: KNOW YOUR WORTH

"I have been crucified with Christ and I no longer live but Christ lives in me." Galatians 2:20

The previous heart reflection was so powerful for me; it impacted my heart so that I will never be the same. I share with you an entry from my journal, a dialogue with my heavenly Father as my heart continued to embrace the value and worth He has placed in me … and in you. My prayer for you is that the love of God enfolds you, the power of God frees you, and the healing of God fills you!

> Heavenly Father, as I read your Word today (Galatians 2:20), I am again struck by its truth. I am reminded in this verse that I have been crucified with you. It's supposed to be less about my striving (in my flesh) and more of trusting (in my heart). It's about living a holy life not out of fear of punishment but out of love for you.

I realize now how I still strive at times—maybe not so much now to earn your love—but to be perfect and have it all together. I am still misguided that in the perfection is where I will find my worth and value. For it is that which defines me. That lie still has a hold on me. Father, please help me to find balance in this area, as I no longer want this mistruth to have its grip on me. I desire nothing but your truth to define my worth.

Again, I am reminded of Galatians 1:15: "You knew me before I was born." Your value and worth were placed upon me then—long before I had life—and in light of that, nothing else matters. There is nothing left for me to prove or strive for. You knew me then, and that is more than enough for me.

Father, continue to impart this truth upon my heart—allow it to settle deep into the very heart of all I am—so I may fully *know* and *believe* that my worth is found in you. Heal that part of my heart and my mind that is wounded from thinking that what I do defines my worth.

Heart response: Allow your heart to be open to this truth, and in doing so, allow yourself to be made whole.

I mentioned at the very beginning that, although I had a relationship with God, there was always something that eluded me. That is really the heartbeat of my story. I knew God, but I didn't know who I was in Him. I gave my all in raising my children and creating a loving family home. Likewise, with my relationship with the Lord, I wanted to get it all right, and yet doing all the right things still left me feeling empty and incomplete most of the time.

Despite how I was feeling, God was still gracious enough to use me in spite of myself. I got involved in our Women's Ministries group at the church I was attending, and it was there that I began to develop the gifts and abilities God has given to me. Let me share with you a few lessons I learned along the way.

First, God desires humility not only in our day-to-day life but especially in positions of leadership. I learned that quite quickly as I got involved in our women's group. I felt I had a lot to offer (how humble of me!). And yet time after time, I found myself doing what I thought were very mundane and meaningless tasks. Yet it was in this place where I learned about being a servant, to be willing to do whatever God asked, and to do it well and faithfully. I clearly remember our pastor's wife happily reciting the Scriptures: "Whatever your hand finds to do, do it with all your might" (Ecclesiastes 9:10) and "Whatever you do, work at it with all your heart, as working for the Lord, not for men" (Colossians 3:23). That became the difference for me. I knew God was watching me, and I wanted to please Him.

Second, our worth is not found in our title or what we do. Struggling with insecurities and self-esteem issues most of my life, I had always thought if I could just be this or that, then I would be good enough and would have arrived.

35

That mind-set followed me for many years. Nothing could have been farther from the truth. I believe God purposely kept me in a humble place long enough until I learned to desire His will and nothing else. I can remember sitting in my pastor's office with the leader of our Women's Ministries group, Mary, who was also a dear friend. At the time, I was her assistant. I don't remember all the details, but during our conversation, she suggested to the pastor that I be the next Women's Ministries leader. My stomach hit the floor, and yet at the same time I felt peace as God was saying, "This is your time for me to use you." Leaving the meeting, I said to Mary, "I really don't know if I can do this." Her reply was, "That is exactly the place God wants you in." There was such truth in that statement, and I have gleaned much from those words. God desires us to be willing to come to him with no plans of our own but just an open heart that is willing to serve Him and be used for His glory. It took quite a few years for me to learn that lesson, but once I did, it brought such freedom to my heart and life.

God finally began to break through my feelings of emptiness and unworthiness during a communion service. After communion was served, the pastor invited us to spend some time down at the altar. As we did, he also encouraged us to envision ourselves sitting at the feet of Jesus and to rest our heads against our Father's lap. That was not something I was accustomed to doing, but I found myself desiring to rest in my Father's arms. In the quietness of the moment, I did just that. I saw myself sitting at the feet of Jesus, leaning my head against Him, and I heard Him speak my name! Not audibly, but there was such an impression made upon my heart that it took my breath away—for in that moment, I realized that the Lord really knew me. To hear Him call my name brought an immediate healing to my heart—I was known by my heavenly Father.

That was when I began my search to discover who I was as His child. Also, it led me to discover the worth that came with it. Stop and think for a moment about the people who *really know* you well in your life. Those you know well are most likely people of great importance to you and that you care for dearly. It works the same way with God, for those He calls His own are of great worth in His eyes. For that reason alone.

My friend, I have come to learn and know for certain that our worth comes from being the "dearly loved children of God" (Ephesians 5:1) that He created us to be. Period. End of sentence. Nothing we do will make us good enough or make God love us more. In Christ, we are all we need to be: complete, good enough because of God's sacrifice of His Son, forgiven, and loved because of Christ's shed blood. Stop striving in your own strength, receive all God has for you, and start standing in the truth of who you are in Him.

In God's perfect timing, I became the coordinator of our Women's Ministries group, and it was during these years that I became more aware of the gifts God had given me. It was in this position where my passion for encouraging women in their walk with God began, and it continues to this day. There was no greater joy than sharing with other women what God was showing me in my very own life, and in doing so, trying to be a vessel of encouragement.

During these times, I sat under the discipleship of my pastor, Manzer Wright, and gleaned so much from his ministry. I was like a sponge soaking up all the wisdom I could find. His preaching greatly challenged my walk of faith, and I know it has played a major role in who I am today. He has gone on to his heavenly home, but I stand as a life changed by his teachings. They were the foundation of my relationship with the Lord.

Chapter 6

HEART REFLECTION: DIRECTION— FINDING YOUR WAY

"Your word is a lamp to my feet and a light for my path." Psalm 119:105

I just love my GPS! I used it recently as I was heading to a new location. I plugged in the address and it just told me where to go—"Turn left," "Turn right," etc.—till I arrived at my destination without any hitches. It was an enjoyable ride. This got me to thinking …

Just like a GPS can tell you what direction to go in, recalculate when you make a wrong turn, and help give you an alternate route, God's Word does the exact same thing for our lives. His Word "shows us truth, exposes our rebellion, corrects our mistakes, and trains us to live in conformity to God's will, in thought, purpose, and action. Through the Word, we are put together and shaped up for the tasks God has for us" (2 Timothy 3:16, The Message).

His Word is *vital* to the direction our lives take. God was revealing to me that I needed to be more consistent about reading

His Word. More specifically, I needed to read it and *apply* it to my heart and life. In order for healing to begin and for freedom to take up residence in our hearts, God's Word, first and foremost, has to be our very heartbeat. His Word needs to be the solid foundation for us to build our lives upon. We need to believe that Scripture, God's Word spoken directly to us (you personally), is true and that every promise is for you.

Allow the truth of these Scriptures to permeate your heart and mind:

- "All your words are true" (Psalm 119:160).
- "In the beginning was the Word, and the Word was with God, and the Word was God" (John 1:1).
- "The grass withers and the flowers fall, but the word of our God stands forever" (Isaiah 40:8).
- "And we also thank God continually because, when you received the Word of God, which you heard from us, you accepted it not as the word of men, but as it actually is, the Word of God, which is at work in you who believe" (1 Thessalonians 2:13).

Heart response: As you allow the truth of God's Word access to every area of your heart and life, let me ask you a question. How will your direction change?

I remember sitting in a Sunday school class and sharing a verse of Scripture from Jeremiah 29:13: "You will seek me and find me when you seek me with all your heart." I truly believe this was the beginning of a fresh hungering after God in ways I never had before. This Scripture birthed a newfound desire to seek God more than I had been and gave me the assurance that when I did, I would find Him. Looking back now, I still wonder if it was just another attempt on my part in trying to get it all right, to do the right thing. In other words, if I could just do *this*, God would be pleased with me. It only stands to reason that because of my desire to please others, I desired to please God as well. Sounds like a good thing, right? Or is it? The answer depends upon your motivation. Is it love for God, or are you fulfilling an emotional need in yourself to please? That is where I found myself. Despite my earnest desires for God, something was always missing. Not only did my heart not have the right motivations, but it needed to be healed.

When I was younger, I had a lot of baggage. Along with my people-pleasing character, I had insecurities as well. I was very insecure, always struggling with low self-esteem and self-worth. I never thought I was good enough, and I had fear of rejection as well as a fear of failure. I had to be wanted, needed, and loved. All of these insecurities led me to live a very performance-driven life, and it was in living that way that I found the little self-worth I had. The overwhelming desire for acceptance and love was a tall order for anyone to fill ... my family, my friends, and eventually my husband and children!

Please don't get me wrong. God *is* pleased when we do the right thing, and there is nothing wrong in doing the right thing. But it is more about the motive behind what you are doing.

Why are you doing the right thing: to be loved or to receive acceptance? Or is it out of love, out of a heart to love God and others? Most of the time, my motive was to be loved and accepted. If you have ever experienced the disappointment of trying so hard in life to please those around you, only to see your efforts bring no satisfying results, you know what I am talking about.

Let me stop here to encourage you. I know exactly how you feel. Please listen carefully ... *God loves you just the way you are.* Okay, you read that too quickly. Pause for a moment and take in each word. "For God so loved the world (*you*) that He gave His one and only son, that whoever believes in Him shall not perish but have eternal life" (John 3:16). You may have heard that Scripture before, or maybe you are reading it for the first time. I heard that Scripture most of my life, but it was all head knowledge. The truth of that statement and the impact of that Scripture never fully penetrated my heart. For years, I lived for the love, acceptance, and approval of other people. I defined myself by it. When I came into a relationship with Jesus Christ, I then lived for the love, acceptance, and approval of God. I strove for it. It took many years to realize that what I sought was mine all along. It was not based on anything I could do but simply because I was His child. Once that relationship is established, the truth of God's Word will find its home in your heart and change you. It will be the beginning of a freedom you have never known before. Seek Him, and you will see the transforming power of God's Word as it loosens the chains of lies and unbelief that have been wrapped around your heart. That, my friend, is the truth!

We were members at our church for eighteen years, and I share the following only because I believe it plays an integral part in my journey in developing *a heart to know Him.* God uses *all* the circumstances we go through for our ultimate good. We started attending a new church when we were married, and we raised our two children there. As infants, they were dedicated to the Lord and they both surrendered their lives to Jesus at a young age. As a family, we were all baptized in water together. Our church truly had become family to us. It was with tremendous sadness and pain that we decided for the sake of our family to leave our church home. Suffice it to say, we know that, "In all things God works for the good of those who love Him" (Romans 8:28). The truth of those words would not become a reality to me until years later, but I can look back now and see He worked it all for good. I wouldn't be where I am today without having gone through that heart-wrenching time.

This was one of the lowest times of my life. I felt like my whole world had been pulled out from underneath me. The details of what happened are not important, but let me say that people are human beings and, as is often the case, people disagree about beliefs and the proper direction for a church. And those disagreements can become very contentious. The more people voiced their opinions, the more difficult things became. Sides were drawn and the church fractured.

The rejection I felt, even though we were the ones that had left the church, had been enormous. I was experiencing a depth of pain I'd never imagined. My faith was shaken to its core, and I was left with trying to pick up the pieces and find God in it all. Although nothing had happened to us directly, indirectly my husband and I felt we were in the minority in how we were feeling about issues going on in the church. After being at this church for eighteen years, it was like going through a gut-wrenching divorce or untimely death. The pain was in the sudden change our lives were now taking. Everything we had known and were familiar with in regards to our church and church family came to an abrupt end. I shut down in many ways and experienced moments of depression and loneliness. During this time, I came across a quote: "Dance like no one is watching, and love like you've never been hurt." I love that quote because it is good advice, and yet at the same time it is very difficult to live out. It caught my attention because I knew it meant I had to risk once again being vulnerable and loving others … Heartache, pain, disappointment, and change are inevitable in life, and I believe as difficult as it is to risk again in any way, we will never experience the fullness of all God has for us unless we do. We need to know that our heavenly Father is with us through it all. "He knows the way that we take" (Job 23:10).

For a few weeks, we just stayed home on Sundays. We didn't know where to go and we were so broken we just needed time. After that brief time, we realized that we needed to be about finding another church. Having a preteen and teenager at the time, it was important to us to get our children in a healthy Christian environment as soon as possible. All of that brought us to the church we now attend and have attended for ten years.

In the beginning, we just went through the motions, all for the sake of our children. Looking back, I don't know if we set the greatest example for them. Our pain was so raw at the time; it was just about getting through, and for the next three years, I continued to do just that—go through the motions.

I got involved in a wonderful Bible study within a year, but I felt like I'd take one step forward and two steps back. Change doesn't come easily for me; actually, I strongly dislike change, so everything was a struggle. I recall walking around in a lot of pain and disappointment and the last thing I was going to do, or felt like doing, was to be vulnerable again. I wasn't anywhere near being able to risk again. So the wall went up, and I kept it up for about three years. Thankfully, I was surrounded by a lot of grace-filled people who extended nothing but unconditional love. I know that through those people, God began His healing in me, but all the while, my façade remained.

In my personal walk with the Lord, I was struggling and trying to wrap my head around all my family had gone through. Through my journaling, I was trying to make all the pieces fit. I would cry out to God to restore my faith and hope.

At this time, my husband and I were hearing wonderful sermons that ministered healing to our hearts and mind. It was like our pastor knew all that we had gone through and what we were still experiencing. He was speaking directly to us! So many Sundays, the sermons were tailor made for us.

It was at this time our church began reading *The Purpose Driven Life* by Rick Warren. That was very timely for us and continued us on our journey of healing. It spoke to so many of the broken places we were in, and I truly found myself being amazed at how what we were hearing applied so perfectly to where we were in our own lives. That is just like God!

It took a long time to heal. I took a few detours along the way. It was the beginning again of finding my way back to God. Looking back now, I am overwhelmed at the love and grace God was pouring out to us, but at the time, I was not willing to acknowledge it. Had I done so, I would have to acknowledge God at work in our new situation. But deep down, amidst all the pain, I found myself wanting to go back. Today I know, without a shadow of doubt, I would not be where I am now without this painful experience. Remember my friends, "Weeping may endure for a night, but *joy* comes in the morning" (Psalm 30:5 AMP). There is a time for "weeping" but after that, God rains down the "joy"! God sees all the heartache, the pain, and the brokenness and beckons us to come unto Him and allow His spirit to minister to us.

As my husband just reminded me in a current situation we are going through, sometimes what is good or of value is often birthed in pain!

HEART REFLECTION:
DISCIPLINE OF THE HEART

"We did not give into them for a moment, so that the truth of the gospel might remain with you." Galatians 2:5

The book of Galatians was instrumental in bringing healing to my heart. In the chapter referenced above, there is discussion about "the Jewish teachers, posing as Christians who had somehow been secretly brought into the church and were giving false teaching."[6] Paul responded to the discussion with the above verse, saying, "We should not give into them (the false teachers and false teaching) … not for a moment, so that the truth remains with us!"

As I read that verse, it occurred to me that we must do the same when the Enemy comes to attack us, when our brokenness stirs up negative thoughts and emotions. As Christian believers, we are constantly in a battle. There is an Enemy of our souls, "the adversary, who prowls around like a roaring lion, seeking someone to devour" (1 Peter 5:8). Satan doesn't want us close to

God. He doesn't want God's glory shown through us. He doesn't want us healed, whole, and restored. He is out for one thing only: our destruction.

I don't know what has caused your broken heart not to believe all that God says that you are and has promised to you. But I do know that all the baggage that may come with it is nothing more than distractions from where God wants to bring you. It is a battle we fight in our minds, and it's not easy. We need to be disciplined in what we allow into our hearts and minds that is contrary to the truth of God's Word. It is a discipline in our thought life to think and act differently and a discipline to be obedient to our heavenly Father and His Word. He only desires the best for us!

Heart response: May the truth of God's Word remain active in you. What discipline of the heart is God revealing to you? Do you control your thought life, or does it control you?

When we suffer from emotional hurt—a heart that has been misled, hurt, or disappointed, or is vulnerable or insecure—we will struggle with thoughts, emotions, and behaviors that at times will bombard us and threaten to snuff the very life out of us. I have battled with them enough to know that it takes a discipline of the heart, mind, and will to think differently. It takes effort. It takes "deliberate acts of our will to shift our focus from all that begs to differ with the great truth of the living God"[7] (Beth Moore).

For me, shifting my focus means to make a deliberate act to dwell on the promises of God, to dwell upon those Scriptures that deal exactly with what I may be thinking or feeling at the time. This is another reminder about how important it is to know what you believe. Even more important is to *believe* what you know. Get into God's Word and allow its truth to be active and alive in your heart and life: "The word of God, *which is at work in you who believe*" (1 Thessalonians 2:13). Believing God's Word, which holds His promises for you, is where the healing of your heart will begin. The healing begins when we start to apply the truth of God's Word to our painful experiences. And as we continue to do so, our lives and behaviors change in response to what we are learning and believing. Your heart will begin to *know* Him.

Belief is a discipline as well. Developing a heart that knows God, simply put, takes *trust*. That is the issue for all our brokenness. Believing is not just simply thinking something in your head. The Bible sees belief as more than that. Belief is the conversion that engages our hearts, which in turn change our behavior. That is where my healing began, when all I knew to be true in my head shifted to my heart and I began to *believe* and live out my newfound truth.

I still live out my healing every day. It takes discipline. I do a lot of thinking while I'm driving, and I must say that it is not always constructive and can be rather mindless. Recently, I had one of those days while driving and I allowed some situations to get the best of me. It is in this scenario where I'm vulnerable to old thought patterns and hurtful words spoken to me that want to play in my mind. On good days, I can say, "Sorry, I can't play today!" and on not-so-good days, I allow them full access to take control. When this happened recently, I realized that I just had to take a moment to stop, pause, and lift my thoughts to God—to remind myself that "even before I was born He knew me." When I am able to do that, it brings me much comfort, but I have to make a deliberate effort to do just that. It takes continuous discipline.

When we become disciples of His Word, our hearts will become sensitive to anything contrary to it. For example, there are days when I feel much confusion. When I do, I need to stop and ask myself, "Who is the author of confusion?" Not God, so I know that thought has to go. There are days when I have great anxiety, so I ask myself that same question. The answer is *always* the same. And although we *will* feel all these emotions over our lifetime, we cannot allow ourselves to live in them. We can't camp in them. I did for many years, and it is still a struggle at times. The more disciplined I am in His Word, the easier it is to feed each emotion its proper truth.

Before my husband and I starting dating, a mutual friend of ours approached Paul and asked him what he thought of me. His response was, "She's moody and she wears glasses!" Guess it wasn't love at first sight for him! All these years later I still tease him mercilessly for his response, but the truth is he was accurate in his answer. I did wear glasses, which he wasn't a fan of (but guess who wears them now!), and I was moody. No, you don't understand—I was *really* moody. I could be happy-go-lucky one moment and, if someone ignored me or said something to annoy me, my great mood was over! I lived my life by my emotions. I can still remember my days as a teenager, waking up each morning deciding what mood I wanted to be in, based on how I was feeling. I feel sorry for those who crossed my path during that time. Not my proudest moments.

As I think back on that time, I see how my insecurity played into my moodiness and my fly-by-the-seat-of-your-pants emotions. I was desperate for love and approval, and my emotions fueled the fire of those misplaced desires.

As I have grown in my relationship with the Lord, I have learned that our feelings can be deceitful and they rarely portray an accurate picture of our circumstances. The storms of life can cause us to doubt who we are in God, and the waves of our emotions can shake our faith. It takes a deliberate act of discipline to not be carried away by our emotions but to be led by our faith in God and what He can do.

"*Choose today* whom you will serve" (Joshua 24:15, NLT). Each day we are given a fresh start to *choose* again how we will live. It takes a discipline of the heart to stay rooted in God's Word, seek the mind and thoughts of Christ, and to not fall prey to the disillusionment of our emotions and the tactics of the Enemy. These three things I have found helpful:

1. Keep the communication between you and the Lord ongoing throughout your day.
2. Have someone to be accountable to.
3. Keep your heart and mind hidden in the Word of God.

Chapter 8

Heart Reflection: Freedom of the Heart—Forgiveness

"Be merciful, just as your Father is merciful." Luke 6:36

Forgiveness is a topic that I have studied over the years, and still, at times, I feel like I haven't fully grasped the concept. What I mean by that is I know the *meaning* of forgiveness, but *living* it out continues to be an ongoing process.

I have come to understand that forgiveness is more for ourselves than about the one we need to forgive. For when we don't forgive, we are bound up and imprisoned with walls of anger, bitterness, and resentment. It can be very ugly. Dare I say that many of the issues, struggles, and problems we have in our own lives may somehow be linked with a lack of forgiveness on our part? This isn't a blanket statement, but I have found it to be true in my own life. The hurts we hold onto over the years are damaging to us—they limit us in our ability to commune with God and others. Often we don't realize that this is what's keeping us from being all God intended us to be. Lack of forgiveness on our part will seep into every area of our lives.

God has revealed to me that there is nothing better than being free. The word *free* means "to be relieved or rid of pain or obstacles, to release from imprisonment or restraint." Some other definitions of *free* are these: "let off the hook," "pardon," and "release." When we are free—released from restraint or relieved from pain—we are able to embrace all that God has for us. When we experience freedom, there *is* no better place! Forgiveness plays a key role in bringing about freedom of the heart. Jesus instructs us to *keep on forgiving*. That isn't always an easy feat. For what He has graciously poured out on us, He asks that we in turn do the same to others. The best part is that He never asks us to do anything that He will not equip us to do. Forgiveness is a process; it's a daily discipline. It starts with willingness, and initially, that may be all we have to give. When we bring that to God, He can then empower us with the ability to forgive. Once we arrive at that place, *He is more than able* to work in our hearts, loose the chains that have bound us, and set us free.

Heart response: I pray that as Jesus has forgiven you, you in turn will extend the same forgiveness to others and set yourself free!

In talking about forgiveness, the story of Joseph and his brothers is a very common example that is used. If you are not familiar with it or haven't read it in a while, I encourage you to read it. As you do, I pray that its truth brings healing to your heart (Genesis 37).

Recently, I heard something about Joseph that really resonated with me and helped me in my journey of forgiveness. Joseph was mistreated by his brothers, and he endured unjust imprisonment, but with all that happened to him, he just kept doing his best for God. That nugget of truth found its way to my heart. In the process of forgiveness, we need to keep on doing our best, keep doing what God has called us to do, and keep our eyes on Him. And when we do, *I know* He will complete His work in us.

Remember God uses everything that happens to us, even those things that were intended to harm us, to make us more like Him. Sheila Walsh, Christian author and Bible teacher, says it best: "When you finally understand that God is in control of everything, you don't have to hold grudges or be bitter and unforgiving. If you really trust God you can say I know God meant it for good."[8] What a revelation that is! This truth may not keep you from experiencing the feelings your circumstances may bring, but it does help you to look at them through the proper lens.

There may be situations where you long to hear the words "I'm sorry" or "Please forgive me." Unfortunately, we may never hear them spoken to us and our hearts are left to find their own closure. In these times, we need to turn to Jesus and allow Him to give us what our hearts long to hear, allow Him to clean our wounds, and apply His healing balm.

Even when we find it hard to forgive and are desperately trying to get there, we can give our desire to God. He will honor our yielding to Him and begin the work in us. Often an action and our willingness are the first things we need to offer to initiate the act of forgiving. Our feelings will then follow.

In our continuing struggle to forgive, we need to remember that we are human. We may never *forget* the hurts done to us, but in our attempts to forgive, we need to refuse to allow the pains of the past to influence us in the present.

There have been many instances in my life where I needed to forgive. I am also sure there were equal instances where I needed the forgiveness of others. There is no way around it: forgiveness is hard and downright painful at times, and even more so when you feel you are the one that was wronged. Please understand what I'm about to say in that context.

Whether or not we were the cause of pain or the recipient, we need to forgive—if not for anything else but ourselves. Forgiveness is really for us anyway. In forgiving, we free ourselves from the pain we have been carrying around. In most cases, the other party or parties have moved on while you have been stuck in the prison cell of your pain, bitterness, and resentment.

It also affects our relationship with God. Scripture says that if we do not "forgive men their sins, your father in heaven will not forgive your sins" (Matthew 6:15). So we need to forgive to keep our heart in tune with God. Not forgiving keeps us from experiencing joy, which is the confidence in knowing that God is in control regardless of our circumstances. Ultimately, we are the ones that lose out. We know we have begun the process of forgiveness when we have made a choice to not allow what has happened in the past to affect our relationship with God and those we need to forgive.

Like Joseph, we need to keep on working at forgiving. We need to keep yielding our will to His so He can heal our hearts, and we need to keep on doing our best for God.

I would like to add that it is never too late to offer forgiveness. It's never too late to speak words of healing to someone. I had that experience recently.

A memory came to mind that stayed with me long enough to know I needed to act. It was regarding my daughter Katie. When she was born, she was blessed with beautiful curly hair. Well, not initially. It took quite some time to grow in, but when it did, she had a head full! Her curls posed quite a difficult task every morning in getting her ready for school. It was just a head full of knots, and no detangler known to man helped. Nor did my lack of patience and compassion! I can recall quite vividly her standing in front of the mirror with tears streaming down her face as I was trying to brush through her curls. Suffice it to say, I didn't earn the mother of the year award for this one!

It was this memory that compelled me to talk with my daughter about it. Now mind you, she was a young adult by now, but I still felt a need to apologize for my behavior. My husband has always encouraged me that, when things like this come to mind, I should act on them. It is usually the Holy Spirit nudging you. So I acted. We were driving in the car one day and I thought it was a great opportunity to talk with her about it.

Through a somewhat unsteady voice, I shared that memory with her and told her how very sorry I was for my lack of patience and compassion and how I wished I had shown more love. She started to laugh, as I think the moment was a bit too serious for her. She told me I didn't need to apologize and, more importantly for her, she told me she was more upset about the time I had thrown a hairbrush at her American Girl doll and broke its head! We both shared a few laughs over that!

Whether or not I got the response I was looking for from my daughter doesn't really matter. I acted on something I knew

I needed to do, and even though my words to her may not have appeared to mean much to her at the time, I know words of forgiveness have the power to stay with you long after they have been spoken. Don't ever think it is too late to say you're sorry or extend forgiveness to someone.

You can be certain that when our heart is open to forgive, God moves in powerful way. The beginning of 2005 was such a time that is frozen in my memory. The events that took place at that time were the catalysts for seeing God move in my life like never before.

It was after the New Year, and I was reading a devotional from *The Purpose Driven Life*. It grabbed my attention as it spoke about the New Year being a great time to reexamine your life, and that was right up my alley! It went on to say that the New Year brings new possibilities and opportunities for growth. I found my heart saying, "Yes, I'm ready for any new possibilities and opportunities God wants to bring my way!" The next sentence is what really touched my heart, and I knew when I read it that God was beginning a new work in me. The sentence read, "I'm sure God wants to do *great things in your life*."[9] A simple statement, but after the drought I had experienced after leaving our old church, it was like a cool spring in a parched desert. I knew at that moment that those words were for me. It was a major breakthrough, and it was time! The devotional went on to say that great things wouldn't happen automatically, but that I needed to step out in faith. There was some trepidation due to my fears and insecurities, yet the Scripture that followed in the devotional was the beginning of God birthing a new chapter in my life.

"Plow new ground for yourselves, plant righteousness and reap the blessings *your devotion to me will produce*" (Hosea 10:12, GNT). God was birthing a heart to know Him, and now it came with a promise. To this day, it remains a powerful Scripture in my life. It was time. It was confirmation to me that God wanted to do a new thing and that the haze of heartache and unforgiveness I had been living in for the past three years was about to be lifted.

It was time for a new beginning. *Plow new ground.* My life thus far had been a good one sprinkled with highs and lows, yet I was always plagued with insecurities, lack of self-worth, never feeling "good enough," feelings of inadequacies, the inability to find my own voice, and fear of failure—I'm sure this list sounds familiar to many of you. Year after year of these emotions bearing down on your heart, mind, and soul will wear you down and drain everything from you. I listened to the lies so many times that I started to believe them. It was always easier to be hard on myself instead of turning to God's Word and letting the truth of it restore and renew me.

Plow *new* ground. God wanted to do a *new* thing. In the NIV translation, Hosea 10:12 says, "Sow for yourselves righteousness, reap the fruit of unfailing love and break up your unplowed ground; for it is time to seek the Lord, until He comes and showers righteousness on you." Break up your unplowed ground. My study Bible emphasizes, "Be no longer unproductive [ouch!] *but* repentant, making a radical new beginning and becoming productive and fruitful." How thankful I am for His Word. It is life giving and life sustaining. I sense the same conviction now as I did when I first read that verse. I *knew* God was speaking to me because it brought joy and life to a somewhat hardened heart. The time had come to be productive for God, to allow Him to use my life for His purposes. The time had come to forgive and move on from the past hurts that had bottled up my heart. It was time for a radical new beginning—and the healing that would come with it. *A heart to know Him.*

As God's healing began, His plans and purposes began to take shape. My desire to write returned. I believe that when God is at work in your life, you can't help but want to share it. For me, writing was going to be the vehicle which God was going to work through.

So I began to embrace the idea of writing again. And as I did, my thoughts and ideas began to take shape, but I hadn't acted on anything. My dear and treasured friend, Brenda, has always been encouraging me to write, and I must say she was the catalyst in getting me to actually put pen to paper. So with her encouragement as my green light, I began.

I remember hearing a sermon from our pastor at the time, Joel Eidsness. In his conclusion, he stated, "You need to tell your own story." It was confirmation that I was on the right track. I knew it was time to write, so I started with a letter to him. I began by thanking him and sharing some of my story with him. I will share an excerpt from that letter.

> Dear Joel:
> This letter is a long time in coming, but better late than never!
>
> I've wanted to thank you for the *Experiencing God* series you have been doing—I have benefited so much by it and God has used you to speak healing words to my heart and mind and renew my purpose and meaning to my life. The time you spoke on "Experiencing God in Times of Doubt" was a confirmation of what I felt God had recently been speaking to me. Your last point on "the solutions that give rise to faith" was to tell

your story—and that spoke directly to me—hence this letter to you.

I just wanted to share with you a glimpse of my story since we have been attending Walnut Hill. I came to Walnut Hill very broken, emotionally and spiritually. I'll never forget the woman's face that greeted us the first day we attended—a beautiful smile, a warm embrace, and treated us as if she had always known us. God's love was very evident through her and ministered to me even though I remember crying throughout the whole service—I felt like I was grieving a death. Attending a church for eighteen years, raising our family there, being a very active member, and then leaving was a very hard thing for us to do. It was too much for me, and I couldn't' see God in any of it. I don't do change very well, and as bad as things were, I didn't want to embrace this new change. I went through many different emotions, from confusion, to hurt, to sadness, to doubt, to disappointment, to anger, and most recently, forgiveness and acceptance. It has only been within the last few months where I can say that I have come to a place where I can embrace this change, accept it, and see what God has for me now.

My desire to be used of Him to touch lives is as strong now as it was years ago. The saying "Bloom where you are planted" comes to mind, because I am ready to allow God to use what I went through to somehow help others. Although leaving our church was the most recent, I have experienced many broken moments in my life, many that are common to women—loneliness, depression, and despair.

Ever since I was a young girl, I always enjoyed writing and had dreamed of writing a book one day. That dream has become alive again, and I am stepping out in faith to write my story. When you shared your sermon, I knew this is where I was to begin, letting you know how God has used you and His people to bring me full circle again …

It is a blessing to come to Walnut Hill—a church that not only talks of God's love but actively demonstrates it. Many of your sermons have been a part of the healing process I have been going through. Forgiveness and acceptance was the key for me. Even though I knew that all along, I wasn't ready. Thankfully, God was patient with me … I finally came to a place where I was open and ready to allow God and His Spirit to work in me—forgiving what was, accepting the present, and looking forward to what is to come. In doing so, God has brought beauty from ashes. His promise is being fulfilled … "Reap the blessings your devotion to me will produce" (Hosea 10:12).

Thank you for embracing our family from the beginning and making us feel like we belonged.

Chapter 9

HEART REFLECTION: A HEART SET FREE

"In my anguish I cried to the Lord and He answered by setting me free." Psalm 118:5

*E*very now and then, I read through my journals, both past and present. For the most part, I find it so refreshing as I am sweetly reminded of all God has done in my life and His faithfulness to me. Then there are moments when I read about how insecure, needy, and desperate I was that make me cringe! My heart offers up a song of praise, thanking God for His love that has transformed me. Discovering God's heart and believing His love for me have been the shift that needed to take place for Him to grow me as He has.

While I was journaling one day, I felt God speak to my heart so personally that it really was quite impactful. I want to share a glimpse of it with you, as I know God speaks the same truth to all His children. The quote from my journal read,

> Let the past be the past—I am doing a new thing.
> Remember my grace makes all things new. Dwell
> on these things, these truths—My truth—for the

truth sets you free and I want that for you more than you desire it. For whom the Son sets free is free indeed! Be free, My child, loose the chains that bind you. Believe in Me and in My word. Truth brings freedom to your heart and life. Know the truth, abide in My truth, and live out My truth.

My response was this: God's truth is the key to our freedom. When life finds us in situations that have us bound, we need to reflect on His promises:

- Remember *whose* you are. You are a child of the living God who purchased your freedom at a great price.
- Remember who dwells within you: Jesus, the light of the world!
- Remember His Word. We need to line up our thoughts and feelings with the Word of God. If something is true, then we can turn to God for help in processing it and grow from it. If it is false, don't take hold of it! Choose to "not entertain" that thought, feeling, or spoken word to you.
- Remember what Jesus has done for you. Dying, He saved you and carried your sins far away, setting you free from all that you deserve. "For whom the Son has set free, is free indeed" (John 8:36).

Heart response: Pour out your heart to God today. Lay your pain and brokenness down, and allow Him to set your heart free!

It should be noted that a heart set free does not always get immediate answers to our prayers. I do believe that, as we continue to *seek* Him and *be in* His Word, that our hearts will align to what *He has* for us. We will hear His still small voice, and confirmations of the Spirit will stir within us. To confirm God's voice to us, we need to be prepared to step out in faith to what He is calling us to do. We may not see the whole picture, and may not even know how things will turn out, but stepping out in faith pleases God. He will take us one step at a time and lead us accordingly.

What is important to know is that God *sees* the whole picture from beginning to end, and whatever He brings to us, He will provide all we need. This process reminds me of a tapestry that is often used to illustrate this point. The front of the tapestry is beautiful and flawless, and on the back is a mass of threads that make no pattern, going in every direction. The same is true of our lives. We see the "many threads"—our mistakes and detours—yet God just sees the beautiful tapestry. God is in the process of weaving a tapestry of your life and mine. He knows the end result. I encourage you to trust in His leading. Continue to seek Him and allow His Word to abide deep within you.

I am reminded of a conversation about writing that I had with a friend. She enjoys writing herself. As I shared with her my struggles regarding writing, she looked at me and said, "It really is an act of obedience, Lynne." Her words gave me great pause. I realized God was saying to me, "You already *know* what you should be doing. Stop questioning, stop doubting, and just *obey.*" Writing was *my* thing up to that point. That statement shifted my focus so that this was no longer just my hobby but now *His* requirement.

As God reveals His plans for you, step out and move in His leading. I began to be more disciplined in my writing, as I now knew my purpose. I received a lot of encouragement along the way, which was evidence to me that God was at work and wanted me to continue.

A heart set free is a heart that knows the Lord. "And I will give them *a heart to know me*, that I am the Lord. They will be my people and I will be their God, for they will return to me with all their heart" (Jeremiah 24:7). I came upon this verse during Beth Moore's Believing God Bible study that I mentioned at the beginning of this book. God's redeeming work began when He grabbed hold of my heart in that study. It was life changing for me, and that verse has set me on the course that has become my story.

As I wrote down that verse in the margin of my workbook, I added, "Lord, please give me that kind of heart." I was never more desperate for that to become a reality in my own life. I continued a mini word study on the word *know*, which gave me a deeper understanding of what I was asking for. The dictionary defines the word *know* as "to grasp in the mind with clarity and certainty; to regard as true beyond doubt." That was what my heart was yearning for—to *know* and *believe* who God was to *me* with a new clarity and certainty. I had come upon what had eluded me for most of my life. Believing for someone else always came much easier for me than to believe for myself. Somehow, God's promises were good enough for other people, but I couldn't claim them as my own. Or if I did, I did halfheartedly.

Most of my walk with the Lord consisted of *striving* to get it all right. It was all about my self-worth being dependent on what I did, and there was no room for any grace or mercy. Ultimately, the truth was that I really didn't *know* who I was in God, nor did I *know* God with clarity and certainty. As I have shared my journey with other women, I have found that my story is a similar one. I believe this is an area that a lot of women struggle with. They lack knowing who they are as children of God and all the freedom that it can bring to their lives when they do. And men aren't off the hook either! They often struggle with seeing their careers define their self-worth. They also need to experience the freedom that comes with knowing their worth as children of God.

When I was a teenager, I used to help hostess the Christmas party of my father's boss. I was asked to help assist with set up, serving the hors d'oeuvres, and cleaning up. I loved the opportunity. I clearly remember walking around and offering hors d'oeuvres to the invited guests. Each time I asked, "Would you like one?" the reply was, "Yes, please, and who are you?" I introduced myself as Lynne Petrocelli, Frank Petrocelli's daughter. Because of the position and reputation my father had in his company, I was secure and confident in introducing myself as his daughter. The same truth applies to us. When we come to know and believe who our heavenly Father is—that He is the great I AM, the Alpha and Omega, the beginning and the end, that He gave His only Son so that we might live and that we are the apple of His eye—then we can have that same security and confidence through all our life, even in the trials that come our way.

When I finished the *Believing God* study, I read through the book of Jeremiah. I didn't have to read too far when I came across this verse: "Break up your unplowed ground …" (Jeremiah 4:3). These are the same words referenced in Hosea 10:12, which is the same verse God had given to me a few years earlier. I knew God was beginning to connect all the dots, but where was He leading me?

Chapter 10

HEART REFLECTION: GOD'S REDEEMING GRACE—HE MAKES ALL THINGS NEW

"... who redeems your life from the pit." Psalm 103:3

There is something about the word *redeems* that I just love! It resonates deep in my heart every time my eyes come upon it. In fact, it seemed a common theme for all God was doing.

When I think of the word *redeems,* I think of second chances, making better, and claiming something lost. Can you relate to any of those meanings? I sure can. God has been faithful to show me how He can redeem anything that we give to Him. The actual definition of the word means to "change, recapture, reclaim, regain, restore the honor, worth or reputation of." Wow! By this definition, can you look back over your life and see God's redeeming grace at work?

I used to be a big coupon user. I love getting a bargain. The concept with coupons is that in using them, you get something at a better price than you would had you not used them. Sometimes using coupons gets you free products by simply redeeming the coupon. Other times, you can buy one product and get another product for free using a coupon. In each case, using coupons gets you something good—not because of anything we have done, but simply because we redeemed our coupons.

I see God's redeeming grace the same way. God's grace is given to us not based on anything we have done or deserve. He just gives it because of His overwhelming love for us. Through His redeeming grace, He restores those broken moments in our lives and the broken places of our hearts. He gives second chances when we don't deserve them, He reclaims those areas of our lives that have been lost, and, most importantly, He can change any situation in our lives and make it better than it was before.

In the above verse, it is God who redeems our lives from the pit. He takes our lives when surrendered to Him and makes them new.

Heart response: What is the pit you are facing? Are you facing broken moments in your life, places of pain, weariness, loneliness, confusion, anger, rejection, or insecurity? The good news is that God can redeem you from that place. I pray that God fulfills the true meaning of His redemption in you, that you simply accept His grace and allow Him to make *all things new* in your life!

A familiar place of brokenness that I have faced many times in the past was in the area of rejection. During my most recent encounter with it, my heart couldn't have felt more broken—it truly ached. I began to seek the Lord more and more, and as only the Lord can do, He miraculously began to heal my hurt. Not just spiritually and emotionally, but physically as well, by surrounding me with people that truly cared for me.

I recently read a quote by Christian musician and author Tammy Trent: "Never allow someone to be your priority while allowing yourself to be their option. Go where you are celebrated."[10] God redeemed my brokenness and released me to do just that. I am so thankful that He continues this spiritual transformation in my life. The more I give to Him, the more He restores me. Nothing is ever wasted in our lives: the joys and the victories, the heartache and the brokenness, even broken moments of rejection. He uses it all to draw us closer to Himself and make us more like Him, when we allow Him to.

So where was God leading me? He was bringing me full circle. God's redeeming grace was at work in my life. He was restoring my life and making everything new. My heartache and pain now had a purpose. It directed my heart to know my heavenly Father and Savior in ways I never did before. It allowed all my head knowledge to flow to my heart and birth a relationship that was just out of my reach. Years later, when I had come upon that Scripture in Jeremiah 4:3, it not only confirmed all that God had been doing up until this point, but, more importantly, it *reaffirmed* my worth and value in whom I belonged.

The book of Jeremiah will always hold a special place in my heart. When I made that presentation in class about Jeremiah, I realized that I had worth and value through my teacher's praise. Even more importantly, it set me on a path to realize the love and worth I hold in my heavenly Father's eyes. Hands down, that wins! And it was in the book of Jeremiah that I learned a life-changing truth. I could have *a heart to know Him,* and thus the title of my story! I would not be the person I am today, nor would I be where I am today, if not for every encounter, every milestone, every victory, every obstacle, every heartache, and every disappointment. God met me in every one. I sought Him and I pressed in until His heart became my own.

We must never forget that God is in control of our lives. Are you familiar with the book of Job? For all the suffering Job endured, nothing happened to him that God didn't know about or allow. In Job, the Lord said to Satan, "Very well then, everything he has is in your hands" (Job 1:12). This Scripture makes us aware that God is the author of the affairs of our lives. Storms of life, difficult circumstances, painful situations, and moments of brokenness do not touch us without God knowing.

> The words that hurt you, the letter that caused you pain, the cruelty of your closest friend, your financial need—they are all known to Him. He sympathizes as no one else can and watches to see if *through* it all you will dare to trust Him completely.[11]

> God doesn't waste an ounce of our pain or a drop of our tears; suffering doesn't come our way for no reason. He seems especially efficient at using what we endure to mold our character. If we are malleable, He takes our bumps and bruises and shapes them into something beautiful."[12]

The shaping of our bumps and bruises allows us to encounter "full-circle moments" whereby we are able to see how God has worked our brokenness and pain for good.

I am reminded of such a full-circle moment now that I am able to embrace the Father's love for me. My perfectionist qualities made it easy to try to do the "right thing," and in doing so, I thought I could earn God's love. I was in a desperate search for God's love, which often played out during the altar calls at my previous church. That time in the service always ministered to me, and it seemed like I was down there every week. There was always this sense of sorrow for not being good enough.

One Sunday in particular, a woman had come to pray with me down at the altar. After a time of prayer, she looked at me and said, "You have a hard time receiving God's love." I don't recall my reply, or if I even had one, but I do remember being surprised and wondering what she was talking about. In light of all God has been doing in my life, since that moment, it is clear that she was right on target—I just didn't know it yet. The words she spoke had brought to light what had been eluding me. And although it took me many years, God has been at work drawing me to Himself. He miraculously touched me and healed my heart so I could know Him, *really* know Him, and believe Him. And knowing Him also means accepting His Word and His promises as my own.

That has been my journey.

As I look back, God's hand is evident throughout, even if at the time I couldn't see it. I think I may have started out my life believing that the more I did defined who I was and gave me my self-worth. But through this journey of healing, I now know that being God's child means being loved, accepted, and forgiven. This is where my worth and identity lie. My heart has come to desire more of Him and desires to be used of Him more and more, but that no longer defines my worth. My worth and value come not from what I do but in knowing to whom I belong. "I have called you by name and you are mine" (Isaiah 43:1).

If there is an echo that you have heard throughout my journey, that is it: *Remember whose you are; remember to whom you belong.* That is the foundation of your relationship with the Lord.

Chapter 11

Heart Reflection: A Thankful Heart

"I will give thanks to the Lord with all my heart." Psalm 9:1

During the past year, I've had a thing for MRI tubes—not that I've had much choice in the matter. I usually don't get too worked up about having to lie there perfectly still, but recently it was different. The technician was telling me to watch my breathing because that might make me move and blur the images—that got me a little nervous. Of course, when you're told not to do something, isn't that the very thing you find yourself focusing on? I took one breath before the machine started and tried to breathe slowly.

The Christian music I had requested started to play, and I remembered that people were praying for me. My heart was thankful being wrapped in their prayers. In the midst of a not-so-great but could-be-so-much-worse diagnosis, my heart was thankful. Simply put, being thankful can be healing in and of itself. A heart that has been restored, redeemed, and made whole is a thankful heart. Are you in the midst of a trial or trials? Are you weary from being tested on every side? Have you lost hope because you are deep in your circumstances? Has the stress of life just gotten to be too much? Has your heart experienced more loss, disappointment, rejection, and heartache than you can bear?

Being *thankful* may not be the remedy you want to hear. I have found when I don't have any words left to say and feel like I am at the end of my rope that thanking God brings a healing balm to my heart. It shifts my heart and mind from my current place of pain to the faithfulness of God and how far He has carried me already. Being thankful comes from what I know for certain. It is not based on my feelings and circumstances that come and go like the wind.

In the midst of your current circumstances, I pray you can be thankful, because

- God is who He says He is: faithful, loving, gracious, and merciful. "The Lord is gracious and righteous; our God is full of compassion" (Psalm 116:5).
- He loves you. "I have loved you with an everlasting love" (Jeremiah 31:3).
- He will meet your every need. "But my God shall supply all your needs according to His riches in glory by Christ Jesus" (Philippians 4:19).
- He will carry you through. "For I am the Lord, your God, who takes hold of your right hand and says to you, do not fear; I will help you" (Isaiah 41:13).
- His peace and divine strength are with you. "The Lord will give (unyielding and impenetrable) strength to His people; the Lord will bless His people with peace" (Psalm 29:11, AMP).
- He promises healing to you. "He heals the brokenhearted and binds up their wounds" (Psalm 147:3).

Heart response: Take a moment to step outside your circumstances, shift your focus upon the Lord, and tell Him you are thankful.

Thankfulness Requires

① Keeping our eyes on Jesus

② His presence always w/us

③ Praise & Thanksgiving draws us more

As I reflect upon my life up to this point and I look back at my life through the lens of God's tapestry, I know He has made something beautiful out of my life. Not because of anything I have done, but because of His great love and mercy that He bestows upon those who believe in Him—His children. If we truly believe God is in control over our lives, then we can look at all our life circumstances and *know* that what the Enemy meant for our destruction, God delivered us from. And He turned it into good.

Have you ever heard the saying, "There isn't a testimony without a trial or a test"? There is much truth to that statement. Without the trials in our lives, we would be stagnant, unproductive, and lose sight of purpose in our lives. God uses our trials to shape us more into the image of His Son. Everything that has happened in your life up to this point has shaped and molded you into the person you are today. Some of you may be thinking, *That's not a pretty picture.* With Jesus in our hearts, He takes all our broken moments and uses them to fulfill His purposes in our lives, if we will but just yield to His working in our lives. He alone gives meaning to our brokenness.

Being thankful can be a hard thing to do when you are in the midst of trials, and it is even harder to see any good in the midst of your brokenness. It is in this place that we need to find *something* thankworthy about our situation and thank God for what He has *already* done for us. That is what our thankfulness should be based on—the faithfulness of God. His Word promises, "Being confident of this, that he who began a good work in you will carry it on to completion until the day of Christ Jesus"

(Philippians 1:6). If you can be thankful about anything else, let your heart meditate on that truth.

Being thankful requires us to keep our eyes on Jesus. When we focus on ourselves, we dwell on our own circumstances, pain, people who caused our pain, and our own understanding of what is going on. Focusing on all of that just draws us farther away from God and His presence in our lives.

We want to keep our eyes focused on Jesus. That is how we stay thankful. When we focus on Jesus, we realize that He has given us the power to be triumphant despite our circumstances.

> We are hard pressed on every side, but not crushed; perplexed, but not in despair; persecuted, but not abandoned; struck down, but not destroyed. We always carry around in our body the death of Jesus, *so that the life of Jesus may also be revealed in our body.*
> 2 Corinthians 4:8–10

Jesus is able to shine brightly in us even in our darkest moments, when we surrender our will and understanding to Him. When we focus on Jesus, we realize His presence is with us always. This might take some practice—to become aware that God is with us all the time—but He is a prayer away. "The LORD himself goes before you and will be with you; he will never leave you nor forsake you. Do not be afraid; do not be discouraged" (Deuteronomy 31:8).

Jesus is always with you, even in your loneliest times. He is with you in every moment of every day—He never leaves your side. We need to constantly remind ourselves of this truth until we know that we know that He is. Lastly, when we focus on Jesus, we realize that He has given to us the gift of Himself that dwells within us. As we continue to focus on Him and strengthen ourselves through the power of His Word, He promises to abide in us. "Dwell in Me, and I will dwell in you" (John 15:4, AMP).

One of my favorite worship songs is "Thank You" by the Katinas. It is a beautiful song which simply says, "Thank you," to the Lord for loving us, meeting our needs, and being with us, as well as for carrying us through, for who He is, for saving us, for His peace and strength, for looking beyond our faults, and for showing mercy.

Having a thankful heart for *all* God has done in your life will move you from living in the midst of your circumstances to living above your circumstances, where you know you are being carried by Him.

I now extend my thankfulness to you for coming alongside me in my journey. My prayer is that God's truth and His promises that I have shared will resonate deep within your own hearts and lives, bring you healing, and draw you closer to having a heart that knows Him.

My journey continues. It doesn't end here all gift wrapped with a pretty bow. I would be remiss to allow you to think that. I must share that my healing continues. There are still broken moments, hurts, and disappointments in life. But God is ever faithful to not let go of my hand, and He beckons me to seek Him even more. I'm learning that when we are *so* saturated in His Word and we spend time in His presence, we are then able to surrender to the Holy Spirit. He gives us everything we need to live through our brokenness and pain.

Our circumstances need not define us. Like Shadrach, Meshach, and Abednego, we can go through the fires of our life knowing Jesus is in the fire with us—filling us with joy despite how things may appear.

May you continue on, or even start, your own journey in developing a heart to know Him, our precious Jesus, who is our Lord and Savior. You will be blessed beyond measure.

"You will seek Me and find Me when you seek Me with all your heart ... I will be found by you, declares the Lord" (Jeremiah 29:13).

And when you do ...

"I will give them *a heart to know me*, that I am the Lord. They will be my people and I will be their God, for they will return to me with all their heart" (Jeremiah 24:7).

Afterword
Poured Out and Pressed In

My journey continues; I have not arrived. God continues His work in me. His work continues in you as well. He yearns to draw us closer, reveal more to us, and mold us into His image.

It is with that thought that I share this last word with you. At the completion of this book, my life could not look more unraveled with certain life circumstances facing me. I have felt at the end of my rope many times only to have the Lord come beside me, lift me up, and carry me on.

At times when I feel I am at the end of myself, I often retreat instead of pouring all my heart holds to God, again. When I make this choice, I am exhausted from the toll my emotions have taken on me, and I often leave that time feeling empty and alone.

Recently, someone of wise counsel shared with me a Scripture from Psalm 62:8: "Trust in Him at all times, O people; pour out your hearts to him, for God is our refuge." The part that was emphasized to me was *pouring out your heart to Him*. I had to confess that I don't do that very well. This person suggested that those are the times when I need to "press in." I asked what that looks like exactly and was told the *pressing in* after the *pouring out* is found in waiting to hear something from God and allow His presence to move upon my heart.

This is not necessarily a new truth to me but more of a reminder of a discipline that is desperately needed in my life—not just for the times of trouble and pain but even more so in developing and maintaining a heart that knows God personally. It truly is a discipline to wait upon the Lord—to wait for Him to speak, to comfort and encourage you in your time of pouring out. We need to press in and wait until He comes through somehow: a new insight or truth spoken to our heart, a Scripture that is brought to our remembrance, a song that identifies with our struggle, or simply by His presence. We need to wait until we hear something from God that helps us to know that He has heard our prayers poured out before Him and is involved in working on our behalf.

Nobody likes to wait, especially in our world of instant gratification. We want everything *presto!* But I am learning that this time of *pressing in* before the Lord is where He is truly shaping our hearts to know Him more intimately. It is where we will receive His love, grace, and strength to live through our circumstances another day.

When you pour out all that your heart holds—all your emotions, troubles, and struggles—and then press in to wait and hear from the Lord, I believe it is one of the most profound disciplines that will lead your heart to truly know Him.

With every blessing,

Lynne

Endnotes

[1] Moore, Beth. *Believing God Bible Study*, DVD (Lifeway Christian Resources, 2003).

[2] Dictionary.com. All definitions are taken from Dictionary.com, LLC, 2012.

[3] Roosevelt, Eleanor. *This Is My Story* (Garden City Publishing Co., 1939).

[4] Gurnall, William. *The Christian in Complete Armour,* Vol. 1 (Banner of Truth, 1986).

[5] McGraw, Dr. Phil. *Relationship Rescue Retreat,* 2004.

[6] MacDonald, William. *Believer's Bible Commentary* (Thomas Nelson Publishers, Inc., 1995), p. 1,878.

[7] Moore, Beth. *Believing God Bible Study*, DVD (Lifeway Christian Resources, 2003).

[8] Walsh, Sheila. *Beautiful Things Happen When a Woman Trusts God* (Thomas Nelson, Inc., 2010), p. 154.

[9] Warren, Rick. Purpose Driven Connection, "Daily Hope."

[10] Trent, Tammy. Twitter, @tammytrent, 2012.

[11] Cowman, L. B. *Streams in the Desert* (Zondervan Publishing House, 1997), p. 28.

[12] Peretti, Frank. *The Wounded Spirit* (Thomas Nelson, Inc., 2000), p. 179.

Fear - Faith by The power of Jesus
Jealousy - Contentment -
Anxiety - peace
Guilt - We are forgiven

Bitterness - Contentment + Joy
Unforgiveness - The ability to extend
            forgiveness
Inadequacy - healthy dependence of God

Remember what Jesus has done.

CPSIA information can be obtained at www.ICGtesting.com
Printed in the USA
BVOW011946071112

304945BV00001B/10/P

9 781449 766641